I TALKED TO GOD AND THEY TALKED BACK

I TALKED TO GOD AND THEY TALKED BACK

10 Divinely-Inspired Poems on Love
and Manifesting Your World

Cia Onyā

CIAO AHAVA BOOKS

ISBN: 979-8-9894434-0-6 (Paperback)
ISBN: 979-8-9894434-1-3 (E-Book)

Any references to historical events, real people, or real places are used fictitiously. Names, characters, and places are products of the author's imagination, exceptions being celebrities mentioned by name.

Cover design and art concept by Cia Onyā.
Cover art and cover design implementation by Azure Prince, www.azureprinceinc.com.
Back cover image author's own.

Printed in the United States of America.

First printing edition 2023.

Published by:

Ciao Ahava Books, LLC
P.O. Box 724084
Atlanta, GA 31139

CiaoAhava.com

To John V and our family:

I love y'all peoples, hear?

God <u>do</u> got it,

but not in the way we thought.

JV, I'm so glad you already know

you have the keys to it all.

Keep carefully and credibly crafting your creed.

Mama love him.

Table of Contents

Preface

I am not a writer. Well, in the sense that words were formed in my head, I wrote them down, later typed them up, and adjusted them, I suppose I am what you would refer to as an "author" or "writer."

However, prior to this work, I had not made a living from writing original words under my own name. I'm a paralegal by trade, so any writing or editing credits naturally go to the attorneys with whom I work, as anyone in the legal profession would know.

No, in this case, with this book, rather than words simply forming in my head from "nowhere," my feeling—nay, my *knowing*—is that the words were *given* to me by Others who may not be perceived by the five main physical senses. One might refer to this conglomerate as God, Source Energy, my Higher Self, the Universe, what have you. I am not sure what to call Them or It—even my pronouns are not exact, I feel. We don't yet have a word that would satisfy my personal understanding of All That They Are.

One night—I suppose it was technically one morning in September 2022, as it was somewhere between 12:30 am and 2:30 am—I began a most special meditative session alone. Before this session, I mentally tasked myself with getting a message from Them, an occurrence that I know has happened to others upon undergoing such sessions.

So, once I began to become fully engrossed by the meditation, I immediately picked up my pen and began furiously writing. I could not stop! I wrote the following 10 poems in a row, nonstop. They are in the order in which they were received. Once I would end one, I would immediately get the title and words for the next. Feel the difference in focus, concentration, and clarity between *Falling: Thoughts in the Beginning of Trance* and *Black Women, This is for You*, the respective first and last poems in this collection.

In some ways, I liken my experience with the Source Energy entities to a group of children in a remote part of the world being shown an electronic tablet for the first time. The children may or may not have previously considered the existence of such an object, but imagine many little heads peeking in over this device, pointing, suggesting content, laughing at the results, enjoying, and sharing in the moment. While I was receiving this information, I was the tablet, and They were the children, having so much fun with me, and I with Them.

Because, in addition to my own personality, I was inspired by All-That-Is, made up of an endless number of contributing personalities, many of whom "participated" in inspiring my words that night, we ended up with a succinct book with one message about love, creation and manifestation said many ways and with so many nuances.

The experience was glorious because it felt really good to make the connection with Them so directly, as I had been wanting to do for some time, but I found myself annoyed that I had to keep coming back "down" to form the messages into

English and then into written language and translate that to my hand and to the pen. This little inconvenience was washed over, though, as the night went on, by how amazing the messages were.

As previously mentioned, injected into this work are bits and pieces of my personality, as in where I'm asking myself in *Queen's (Q.O.T.D. + Quid)* for a question to ask to the Universe while I was in this headspace or where I'm describing my relationship with religion as a young girl in *Christian Girl Poem*. You see me going in and out of *Falling*, with references to international superstar Beyonce's addictive late-summer-2022 album *Renaissance* and in my literal line of thought as I was dipping in and out of Heaven, with *Falling* occurring in the beginning of my session, hence its full title.

However, it is to be noted that even in those instances, all of the *essence* of the poems came from Them. Moreover, every bit of advice or direction that you see in this book is from Them. Because I was in the same "receiving" space while writing every poem, I consider this entire book to be given to me by Them. It's just that the messaging had to come through my personal understanding of the world and through my use of the English language, which includes interjections of African American Vernacular English ("AAVE"). Though most of the book is written in Standard American English because my focus for this session was not on AAVE, as I wanted everyone to really understand the overall *message* that They sent us.

Speaking of down-to-Earth messaging, do not be alarmed, but this book contains cursing! [Insert church-lady faint here.]

The reasons for the curse words differ poem-by-poem and line-by-line. In most cases, it serves either to abruptly call the reader's attention to the subject matter at hand or to simply serve as a reminder that God or Source Energy is not concerned about our trivial rules about cursing or other colloquialisms.

The inclusion of cursing tells us that They just want Their message to come to you however it comes and that you be open to receive it. In other words, it's a reminder that cursing will not send you to "Hell." Your thoughts and beliefs can do that for you on their own. Additionally, one or two curse words in this book are actually meant quite literally.

This book is for everybody. I so happen to be a non-religious but formerly-Christian cisgender millennial black American woman in my 30's, but whether you share any of those characteristics or not, this book is for you.

I did, however, at the end of my "session," want to receive a message that was for black women here in the United States or overseas, just because, so I asked Them to deliver a message for us. However, the message is not meant to be exclusionary. It—as with the whole book—is meant to provide guidance where it has been sought by any individual or group of individuals.

It is meant to be read not once but many times so that something new stands out to you each time that you read it. It was written to you, dear reader, with love. Please enjoy.

Pre-tapped Potential

I'm reminded of Ariel
missing her gift, her voice box.
It's how I've been self-taught:
Impotent, stifled ~~creator~~ creature with fire locs.

I have legs to walk
and hands to do
but you really should hear
what comes through for you.

Why haven't I used my voice,
my Higher Sis's desires, wishes?
Witness my attempt to fix this
to flip the script since She insists...

Commence it.

-Cia Onyā

FALLING

Thoughts in the Beginning of Trance

I am light. I am yonder.
I am heretofore and thitherto.
I sway like the breeze
because I *am* the breeze
and it is me.

Whoops! Gone again.

Matrimonial. Patrinonial. Patroniachal? Patriarchy.
What's the message, dear?
Malarkey in hierarchy.
Fear has no place here.

And I'm back.
Don't understand but do, all at once.
Time is fleeting because it
doesn't exist.
How can something persist
which it not is?

This must be how Beyoncé felt,
with a *Renaissance* under her belt.
Riskless. Limitless. Christmas wish list.
You get(tin') this, sis?

This is fun. All day long.
As it should be.
Play. All. Day.

I love it. You love it.
The *real* You, boo,
that's Who.

You're amazing,
making my heart sing
or some shit like that.

Mushrooms, psilocybin...
What the hell have
All-of-I done?

I love you.
You love me.
We're more thrilling
than Barney.
With a great big tub of
oochee goochee goo!
Won't you say you dug me too?

This is the best. I need some rest.
Made a mess of this address.

And it's blessed.

Christian Girl Poem

(AKA How I Wish My Christian Mother Understood God)

Horse. Boat. Parade.
Small towns and old maids.
Took up trite trades,
dug in their graves
searching for souls to save.

Mama made me a ~~slave~~ knave
to behave the King James
until I caved,
an angel caged.

I can't see past you, Mama!
Through all that I do
(and I want to).
You're obscuring my view.

And when I think I'm through
You always come to:
"Be all that is so true,
what love means to you."

A Song of Praise

Whoopty doo-da day!
Singing the day away
Always finding space
to sit and contemplate.

Why, while we are Space,
we hasten to distaste
our neighbor's sweet embrace?

Cotton-candy lace!
Mango-sweet plum!
Pace with all the grace
has brought Us to this place
for which our fathers LIVE
and so do we.
Yet free. Yet in glee.
Whoopty.

Love, Yourself.

Everything is possible.
Be careful what you wish for.
Learn to wish on purpose, "for God's sake!"
Who, besides you, should craft *your* life?
Absurd question! The answer is null.

You are bent by their every word.
Every pixel.
Every airwave.

Get your power back!
You have what's in you!
You are but a mustard seed
among galaxies.
And you *are* the galaxies! All of them.

Don't you see?
You are any- and everything, any- and everywhere, all at once
hence the title [Your Name Here].
It means King.
Every name means King!
In the most gender-neutral way
for there are no genders but One.

Everything is One.
We are all One, for sure.
Be sure.
Come back to Yourself.

Love, Yourself.

3 Kings

Michael Jackson,
Sam Cooke and
Marvin Gaye
all sit on a porch in Heaven.
What the hell do they talk about?!

Michael might say something funny
and all of them laugh.

Then Sam Cooke mocks him with a
"HEE-HOO!" and a *Bad* move,
foot-kick, neck-switch and all.

                    Just wondering.

Queen's (Q.O.T.D. + Quid)

What's something I want to know?
Is this it? Will I have the full backing of the Universe
when it's time to *move*? Is that time now?

Resounding Answer:
YES, GIRL!

It's always a Yes.
Expect nothing less
Primarily because neither nothing nor less
really exists.
Yet all persists.
Endless, it is.

---

500 million quid. Queen's estimate. In tense climate.
Hot temperature, weather- and crowd-wise.
Politically intense.

Should she give it back, posthumously?
This is the question which leaves us weary, leery.

Off-topic, but maybe not really.

500 million quid,
akin to, but beastly compared with
500 million dollars, bangers & mash, sold.
Out loud today to my son I told
of that, my desire,
my end fiscal goal.

When she, dead lady, had
500 million quid worth
of tortured brown and black souls,
holes written into ornate ivory
and shiny, shiny gold
in your hallways.

Yes, gold, ebony, ivory, silver
sitting in a portrait frame,
In. Your. Hallways.
Its only purpose to catch the gleam
of the sun through the floor-to-ceiling
windows once a day,
witnessed by no one.

You killed 900 black slaves per frame,
1000 Indians per vase,
As many natives as thread-count
in all yer linens.

I would say, "Go Heck Yourself," but
that's being too nice.

All Things Together for the Good

It's funny how things tie together.
All things work together for the Good of those that trust THEM.
Them is you, singularly and plural
The All-You.

When I have myopia, lines disappear.
No matter where I look,
how hard I try to find them,
delineations don't exist.
We put them there in "real" life.
"Get real!" we say. "Lines exist."

I am here (and there and everywhere)
to tell you:
Lines exist when you say they do.
Otherwise, they don't.
Nothing is alone.
Everything is together.
Everything is good.

But Seriously, I Want the Money in the Bank

LOVE. Okay we get it.
What if we say,
"Fuck all that froufrou shit for a second.
I just want the peace
of money in the bank"?

Then we say, "Just do it!
Whatever you want to do.
Do it in your minds first!
Do it! Now!"

You will experience everything twice:
first in your heart
then measured in mass.

Thoughts weigh heavy with a certain gravitas
But feelings and emotions inhabit EVERYTHING.
Every atom is alive and would be "dead" without feelings.
Feeling is exactly equal to the matter produced.

Thoughts and feelings contain the very "real" physical
plasma of which stuff—real stuff—is made.

Never Say Never

Never say never.
No, really.
Don't say that shit.
Because anything you say can be used against you
by you.

Never in a sentence makes me want to know the rest.
What has you so stressed, as to NEVER…?

Girl, you betta be careful!
It's cliché, but hey,
you attract what you say.

Nothing doesn't exist
to the Universe.

Negation is so small
that the Universe doesn't recognize it.
It's impossible to see.

Be seen by the Universe, on purpose!
Speak forwards, not backwards.
For once, talk about what you want,
never what you *never* do.

Black Women, This is for You

Black Women
I'm speaking directly
from Love to you,
which is, too, love.
En masse, what you tend(ed) to create
is (was) that which you fear(ed).
Create anew: first singly,
then jointly
and through the generations.
You have always had it inside you.
You were *so* strong, *so* big, *so* great,
that to dull your power,
centuries of foolishness
were brought in.
I believe you've learned your lesson and
had your glum.
Start creating on purpose, now,
for fun.
You have always deserved it.
Now and forever.
You were just asleep to Us.
Wake up, sis.

Personal Study Guide

**Complete at your leisure:
you are both the student
and the grader,
so be honest,
take your time,
and have fun!**

Though it can seem like these are the rambling musings of a person gone mad, name two "gems" or important messages you gleaned from this poem, and tell why they stand out to you.

_____

_____

_____

_____

_____

_____

_____

_____

_____

_____

_____

_____

_____

_____

To whom does the "_**You**_" in the last stanza refer?

When the young narrator says "I can't see past you, Mama! ...

You're obscuring my view," what was she trying to see?

_____

_____

_____

_____

_____

_____

_____

_____

_____

_____

_____

_____

What exactly is the narrator grateful for?

What emotion(s) do you sense in the asking of the question

in the second stanza?

_____

_____

_____

_____

_____

_____

_____

_____

_____

_____

_____

_____

_____

In this poem, is the phrase "Love, Yourself." a closing
(a way of saying goodbye, as in a letter) or a command?
How can you tell?

_____

_____

_____

_____

_____

_____

_____

_____

_____

_____

_____

_____

_____

_____

What might be the purpose of this poem?

How can you tell?

_____

_____

_____

_____

_____

_____

_____

_____

_____

_____

_____

_____

_____

Are these two poems related? If so, how?

Why do you think there's a line after the first part?

Read them again and pause to examine how your gut feels

after reading each part. Write down thoughts.

_____

_____

_____

_____

_____

_____

_____

_____

_____

_____

_____

_____

If "everything is together" and "delineations don't exist," this means there's no separation between you, your thoughts/beliefs, and your environment.

Look around you right now and notice the environment

of which you are a part.

You attracted everything you notice. Write down your first thoughts about this revelation as it relates to the people and things you see.

_____

_____

_____

_____

_____

_____

_____

_____

_____

_____

_____

What's your version of "money in the bank,"

that is, something you desire right now?

What would it feel like if you had it?

_____

_____

_____

_____

_____

_____

_____

_____

_____

_____

_____

_____

_____

What are some areas in which you catch yourself "speaking backwards?"

Give specific examples. Now change those statements into "forward" statements.

For example: That car accident looked awful; I'd never want that to happen to us! ➔

Thank God for safety at all times for my family and me!

_____

_____

_____

_____

_____

_____

_____

_____

_____

_____

_____

_____

Who do you think introduced "foolishness" into lives of black women?
Why was this allowed? Are black women helpless, given their past?
Who is "Us" in the penultimate line?
What's the importance of creating "for fun?"

_____

_____

_____

_____

_____

_____

_____

_____

_____

_____

_____

_____

www.ingramcontent.com/pod-product-compliance
Lightning Source LLC
Chambersburg PA
CBHW021005150626
46549CB00012BA/1309